To my parents. Without your support,
I wouldn't be who I am today. —Z.L.

For Lee, my #1 reader. —H.D.

To my parents, Hana and Ali. —S.A.

NOT YET

The Story of an Unstoppable Skater

Written by **ZAHRA LARI** and **HADLEY DAVIS** ✳ Illustrated by **SARA ALFAGEEH**

Orchard Books
An Imprint of Scholastic Inc.
New York

The air-conditioned theater is as cold as a rink.
On-screen, a skater spins.
Zahra watches, dizzy with delight.

The skater jumps and twists twice.
Zahra's wide brown eyes grow wider.
In a blink, the skater's blade scrapes back onto the ice.
She smiles.
Zahra smiles back.

That night, Zahra slides down the hallway in her socks.

Left foot, right foot. Left foot, right foot, until she reaches her room.

Asleep in her bed, Zahra dreams.
She skips through warm sand and finds an icy oasis.

Zahra glides across it.

At breakfast the next morning, Zahra's cereal swirls in the milk.

She chases it around
the bowl with her spoon.

"I'm going to be a figure skater," Zahra announces to her brother on the way to school.

"That's ridiculous," he replies. "You don't know how to skate!"

"*Not yet,*" Zahra corrects him.

In the cafeteria, Zahra's best friend, Sumaia, shows off a skirt she sewed. "Cool! Can you make me a skating costume?" Zahra asks.

"You didn't tell me you were taking lessons!"
Sumaia says, surprised.
"I'm not. I mean, *not yet* . . ."
Zahra's face feels hot.

Back home, Zahra has an important question.
"It's about skating," she explains.
"I have a question first," her mom replies,
barely looking up from her book.
"Have you finished your homework?"

Zahra sighs, "*Not yet.*"

"Besides, Zahra," her uncle says frostily,
"figure skaters don't look like you."
Zahra's wide brown eyes fill with frustration.
"*Not yet*," she whispers.

Zahra's dad whispers back.
"Not yet," he agrees.

On Saturday, Zahra's father
takes her to the city.
Soon she's balancing in
bright white boots.

"What do you think?"
her dad asks.

"They're beautiful," she beams.

Zahra zips toward the ice where . . .

A class of kids wiggles backward, leaving lines like squiggles.

A girl her age crosses long limbs, one over the other.

Two teenagers turn like tops.

Zahra can't wait another second!
She steps onto the smooth surface and —

She falls.

And falls again.

And again.

The ice is harder than Zahra imagined.

Skating is harder, too.

Zahra's arm aches.

Surely she'll have a bruise — just like her grandmother said.

Zahra's cheeks sting.

It *is* freezing — just like her grandfather said.

Zahra looks around.

No one is dressed like she is — just like her uncle said.

"Had enough for today?"
Zahra's father calls out.

Zahra's wide brown eyes flood with determination.

And then . . .

left foot,
right foot.

Left foot,
right foot.

Zahra answers —

AUTHORS' NOTES

When I was eleven years old, I saw the movie *Ice Princess*, and I begged my parents for a chance to skate. Skating sounded like a strange idea because I'm from the United Arab Emirates, a desert country with only one skating rink! Just like in this book, my father was the person to grant me my wish. Dad knew so little about the sport, he first bought me hockey skates instead of figure skates!

I finally started lessons at age twelve, which is late to begin skating seriously, but I was determined. I woke up at 4:30 a.m. to train before I went to school, and then after classes I went back to the rink!

As part of my Muslim tradition, I choose to be "covered" in public. This means my skating dresses are long sleeved and designed to be worn with leggings. Over my hair, I wear a matching headscarf called a hijab. The judges of my first international competition, the European Cup, had never seen a skater wearing a hijab. They called it a "costume prop" and deducted points from my score!

I thought that wasn't fair, so I went to meet with a representative from the International Skating Union (ISU). I jumped and spun on the ice, showing that my headscarf was safe to skate in and wouldn't move around or fall off. It worked! They changed the rules!

I am happy to say that although I was the first skater to compete in a hijab, I'm not the last. I believe everyone should follow their dream no matter how far-fetched it sounds out loud. No one will tell you that you're "ridiculous" once you've proven them wrong! Remember, your dream just hasn't come true *yet*.

—Zahra

One morning in Los Angeles, I saw an article about a figure skater from the Middle East named Zahra Lari. I read she was breaking cultural barriers in the sport and even helping Nike design a special hijab for Muslim athletes. *How cool!* I thought. I kept reading and learned this change-making young woman had started skating "after watching the Disney movie *Ice Princess*." I ran to my computer, found Zahra on social media, and typed this message:

"I wrote *Ice Princess*! That my script inspired you to skate, and you've inspired girls all over the world, is the best happily-ever-after *ever*."

Zahra replied within seconds. We became fast friends and decided we had a new story to tell — together. This book is that story.

—Hadley

ILLUSTRATOR'S NOTE

Everything is impossible, until it isn't. I've spent many years as a fantasy artist, but I could instantly see there was true magic to Zahra's story. I felt immediately connected to her, realizing that she had to push through all the obstacles in her way to make her dreams real. Every child has a "Not Yet" moment — no matter where in the world you are, what language you speak, or what your goals may be.

How do you design a character you want your reader to root for? Our first "no" often originates from our fiercest supporters. Our first obstacles are often placed by those who love us most. As I sketched what a young Zahra might look like, I visualized her as small yet able to take up a whole page. Resilience had to dance around in sparkles and tights. Big eyes were needed to represent a bigger heart. As a Muslim woman in hijab myself, I wanted to have some real fun with Zahra's headscarf. I wanted the scarf to fill the page and to wave proudly like a flag whenever Zahra dreamed. The scarf would amplify her beauty, strength, and grace, just as it did in real life.

When Zahra and Hadley first reached out to me with this fantastical story, we wondered if there were any other stories like hers out there. "Not Yet," we said. So, as we reach the end of this book, I hope it is the start of a new story for someone else.

—Sara